The Little Red Handbook of Life

A Guide to Living a Fuller and Richer Life

Vincent Calandra

BALBOA.
PRESS

A DIVISION OF HAY HOUSE

Balboa Press books may be ordered through booksellers or by contacting:

Balboa Press
A Division of Hay House
1663 Liberty Drive
Bloomington, IN 47403
www.balboapress.com
1 (877) 407-4847

Because of the dynamic nature of the Internet, any web addresses or
links contained in this book may have changed since publication and
may no longer be valid. The views expressed in this work are solely those
of the author and do not necessarily reflect the views of the publisher,
and the publisher hereby disclaims any responsibility for them.

The author of this book does not dispense medical advice or prescribe the use
of any technique as a form of treatment for physical, emotional, or medical
problems without the advice of a physician, either directly or indirectly. The
intent of the author is only to offer information of a general nature to help
you in your quest for emotional and spiritual well-being. In the event you use
any of the information in this book for yourself, which is your constitutional
right, the author and the publisher assume no responsibility for your actions.

Any people depicted in stock imagery provided by Thinkstock are
models, and such images are being used for illustrative purposes only.
Certain stock imagery © Thinkstock.

Print information available on the last page.

ISBN: 978-1-5043-7043-1 (sc)
ISBN: 978-1-5043-7042-4 (hc)
ISBN: 978-1-5043-7044-8 (e)

Library of Congress Control Number: 2016919544

Balboa Press rev. date: 11/18/2016

Chapters

To my wife, Moleka, and our three lovely daughters,
Sophia, Isabella, and Arianna. It is my profound hope
that this writing will come to help you in your lives.

Why This Handbook Can Help?

We live busy lives. Such is the case in a modern world. As for myself, I find myself busy with my career; my wife busy with her career; my daughters are busy with both school and extracurricular activities. The day is done in the blink of an eye. We sleep. Then, we get to do it all over again. This is the treadmill of life. Millions, perhaps billions of people live this life.

For the so-called "successful," which I will discuss, the small amounts of open time in their calendar are filled with "things." These things may be the next event, the next party, the next trip, the next school event, the next social dinner, and on and on. Largely, we pretend to have fun in these brief moments, and this is not to say that we do not derive joy from these moments. However, it is quite evident that those who live busy lifestyles are often unable to live in the present and enjoy those items we place on the open slots in the calendar of our life.

We come back from a week of vacation with photos shared on Facebook, and yet for the vast majority of people, this leaves them feeling empty: as empty as the day we planned the trip, took the trip, experienced the trip, and traveled home. This is truth and is the kind of tragedy associated with the modern human experience. Perhaps you stood on the beach to pose for an Instagram photo, yet very little of the experience on the beach "sticks" with you. You stood in front of the Eiffel Tower and captured the moment, but then it was on to the next thing to see, the next place to eat, the next hotel in which to sleep, the airport, and home. Blink. The trip is done. Are you happier? My guess is no. Yes, you added to your life experiences, but largely, while these moments do become memories, we all get right back on the treadmill of life. Sleep, work, eat, and repeat. Repeat and repeat.

If you are fortunate and live into your eighties, you get roughly 30,000 days. We are all mortal, and nothing can change that fact. So, the time you have is an absolute. Perhaps for some, this number is higher, and I hope with all of my heart that you do indeed get to enjoy more days. For some, it is less. Perhaps fewer days are just part of your fate. Perhaps something comes into your life that is unexpected like disease or an accident. Similarly, I hope with all my heart that this does not happen to you. That said, it is a fact that some who read this book will have fewer than 30,000 days, and for some, more. For some, the quality of your life over that 30,000-day period will be better than for others.

This is the reason I wrote this book. Why? It is my simple and very genuine hope that it will serve as a guide to help your life be a far fuller and joyful one, whatever be the quantity of days. That your days, whatever the number may be, will be infinitely better than the step-and-repeat days you are experiencing today.

No one gives you a handbook to life. Your parents, should you be fortunate, did their very best to provide a compass for you. Some will provide a moral compass. Others may provide a direction for your life, based upon their experience and seek to very genuinely help set you on a course that they believe will make you most happy. There is sincerity in most parenting, yet the subject of life for the majority of parents will not be well understood. You see, they in fact are on the treadmill of life trying to raise you and do the very best they can to set you on their personal belief of the "right path." This is the process that happens for the most fortunate of children. Less fortunate children might not be blessed to have loving guidance.

I am not a god nor am I a trained psychologist. I have not run experiments with empirical data that I can show you. I am simply a person. I am, more precisely, a pentagenerian with an accumulation of experiences gained over some roughly two-thirds of those 30,000 days. My wish for you is to absorb the simple advice provided in this handbook so you can avoid my mistakes, put your life on a better and more fulfilling path, and find joy in your days ahead. That's it.

And so, I give you the gift of life. This is perhaps the greatest gift one human being can give to another. I would like you to envision that through my simple wisdom and truth that I am actually extending your allotted 30,000 days by making them not greater in quantity, but greater in quality. I hope to convey advice that will make your days more meaningful and full. My prayer is that I enriched each and every one of those days in a way that will extend your experience of this life. Read. Understand. Then, go forth and make your life wonderful.

~ Personal Notes ~

5

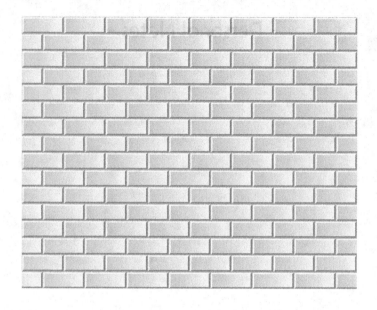

Ego: The Cinder Block Wall

Most parties begin with harmless icebreaker conversation. Nine out of ten times, a person will approach you and say in a benign way, "What do you do?" Most of us have our canned responses ready to go at a moment's notice. "I own a successful landscaping business." "I am a nurse at the prestigious hospital in Boston" (or Dallas or San Francisco or Phoenix, or any one of a thousand other places). "I am a lawyer for Jefferson and Associates." "I am a bank executive." "I am a business consultant with Deloitte running major accounts. "I am a surgeon." "I am a high school mathematics teacher." "I am a senior pilot with United Airlines." "I am a professor at the University of Chicago teaching graduate physics." "I am a director for a prestigious high-tech firm." "I am a hotel manager for Hilton." You get the picture.

From the earliest age, we identify ourselves by what we do and what we own. This is not your fault in the least. Our society places extraordinary value on these things. What mother would not want to say her son or daughter will become president of the United States? What father would not want to say his son or daughter will become the CEO of a multinational corporation? What parents would not want to proclaim from the rooftops that their child is performing research that could bring an end to cancer? It is all very natural and fully aligned with our society's values. And so, we begin to identify with the short elevator pitch of what we are. "I am X, and I do Y, and I own A, B, C, and D—and oh, by the way, I also own two Zs."

What you do translates into what you own and, therefore, becomes the foundation upon which your life is built. Your personal narrative is entirely based upon you being an individual, performing something of value, and translating that into material wealth.

Let's begin the party again. "Hi, I'm Shaun! What do you do?"

"I am a fifty-year-old man with a wife, and we are raising three daughters." Cue the sad-sounding slide trombone. *Wah-wah-waaa* ... You can almost hear the music played on game shows when the wrong answer is given. While the answer given may be factually correct, it is not your best-sounding personal résumé. It does not show the best image of the individual that you have created for yourself in your mind. There are no words in this particular response that show the slightest form of ambition, substance (except perhaps procreation), or achievement. Shaun, our fictional listener at the party, is preprogrammed to screen for keywords that show signs he is speaking to someone of substance. A fifty-year-old man with a wife and three kids is nothing special. He politely states he needs to refill his wine glass, and the conversation is over. *Wah-wah-waaa ...*

When you were born, you were devoid of ego. Simply put, you were perfect in that you were a living creation of the universe, born with a natural curiosity and love for all things around you. This is a state of bliss. There is no façade to defend. There was nothing to compare between yourself and another human being. There was no mental stress. There was no sense of being ahead or falling behind. You were simply alive and absorbing the wonder that was the world around you. That is as it should be.

Now, as time passes, circumstances put you in a position to size up yourself against others and build your so-called ego. Your family lives in a bigger or smaller home. You got an A versus a B in math. You were picked to be in the spelling bee. You sang a solo for the chorus. You were tougher than others and were able to get your way. Teachers liked you, and they were more likely to boost your grades. You were the favored child in your home. You obtained a master's degree.

The cinder blocks of the ego are put in place, and we all build up our own personal walls. That wall is filled with the stuff of which we are most proud. We are then placed in an unconscious cycle to put more blocks in our wall.

We graduate magna cum laude. We earn a PhD. We do research as part of a university grant. We are employee of the month at our place of work. Yes, we are piling up those achievements and cinder blocks that make up the ego.

So, what's the problem? Well, the truth is that most people will never see a problem. Let's play the pattern out. You are successful in school. You get a good job. You earn a paycheck. You see the car you want to own and buy it. You buy a big home. You fill that home with the very best you can afford. You buy a summer home. You travel away to exotic locations for vacations. And more and more and more and more. This is a pattern without end. The ego is hungry and will never, ever be fed enough. It needs the next thing, the next accomplishment, and the next validation that all those cinder blocks are valuable. Our egos force us to chase things that may or may not be part of the true direction of our lives. I want to repeat that: our egos force us to chase things that may or may not be part of the true direction our lives. How do we know this? Have you ever received a promotion and felt empty inside about the longer hours you will have to dedicate to work? Have you ever received a very expensive gift that felt nice but did not make you any happier? Have you ever relentlessly researched for months the next car you will buy until you buy it, sit in it, drive it, and feel no additional joy? Have you ever moved, thinking that your new location or home is going to sweep away feelings of stress and discord, only to discover you are living the same troubled life, but simply in a different location? Have you ever had these empty feelings? The ego wants us to accumulate more, but more often than not, the "more" does not bring happiness or joy.

Let's try something. Close your eyes in a quiet space. No interruptions. Try, in that moment of inner peace, to separate yourself from your ego. Tell yourself that you are not the sum total of grades, degrees, homes, cars, or vacations that you always seem to identify yourself with. Instead, connect with your true inner self. What do you feel? Does your mind take you to a different place? Do you find your mind telling you, "I wish I spent more time painting like I did in high school," "I wish I lived in the country close to nature," "I wish I did not have this particular job," or "I wish I spent more time with my family"? My bet is that your true, peaceful inner self will have the ability to look right through the cinder blocks of ego and see a more truthful and genuine form of yourself. This is the path you need to follow.

A higher power placed inside each of us specific gifts. You are gifted in some way. Ninety-nine percent of us will be on our deathbeds never having pursued the gifts given to us by a greater power. If you believe in God, then let's call this greater power "God." If you do not believe in God, you should accept that each of us has a unique genetic code that predisposes us to specific physical and mental abilities. Your true joy will come when you align your life with those inborn gifts. There is no other path to a more joyful life. Buying another home? Nope. Having another child? Maybe, if that is what aligns for you. Buying a Porsche? Unlikely. Rather, it is your responsibility, not only to yourself but also to the world around you, that you find your inner gifts and share them with the world. The outcome that diminishes you and the entire world is you not achieving your higher purpose in life. You owe it to yourself and to the powers of the universe to discover and put your gifts to work in the world. This will require that you strip yourself of the ever-hungry façade of ego.

Once you are able to put aside ego, a world of possibilities comes to light. It is a brilliant and holy light. It lifts a burden from your shoulders. You no longer have to say and do what others expect. You are, in the most profound sense, free. Free to explore the world in the way that you were gloriously made to experience it. You will get to do this on your own terms. Are you brave enough to separate yourself from years of the cinder block wall you created called ego? Yes. You must be, because therein lies the only path for a sincere and true life for yourself. The universe will see to it that you pursue the gifts that have been bestowed upon you. You cannot fail. There is no such thing as failure once you are on the path of your own inner truth.

~ Personal Notes ~

The Power of the Universe

There is a power accessible to all in the universe. I cannot explain it fully. I have experienced this power in many ways and seen it at work in the simplest and most powerful ways in my life. However, I know for a fact that you cannot access the power of the universe without first stripping away the ego and replacing it with your own inner truth. Once this occurs, you will feel inner peace and the connectedness of all things. You will feel connected to others. You will feel connected to nature. You will feel connected to all things that surround you. That feeling of inner peace is what I can only describe as love. Having put ego aside, you have made room for you to "love" your true self and that path you choose to pursue. You also begin to radiate love. You radiate your inner peace. The people around you will see this incredible power of the universe reborn in you, in your eyes, in your tone, in your appearance, and in your interactions.

You will only be able to access the power of the universe once you no longer see yourself as a disconnected individual. This is the price paid for ego. If you live in the ego state, you are an individual with individual needs, individual wants, and insatiable individual desires continuing in an unceasing way. Ego = Disconnected. Once the ego is gone and you begin to follow the path the universe meant for you, you will immediately feel your unquestionable connectedness with others, animals, nature, the earth, and the infinite universe.

How do I know there is such a power in the universe? I happen to be writing this section on an airplane on my way from Boston to Texas. I have cleared my mind of ego and feel my place of inner sincerity and peace. I can feel myself completely energized. I feel an inner love, or perhaps better stated, a complete and total inner peace. Now, just as I started to write this paragraph, I mentally was in this state of mind and purely mentally suggested to the lady next to me, offer me a pretzel. Yes, I know it sounds absurd but stay with me. I just said to my inner self, "This looks like a very nice lady. I wonder if she would offer me a pretzel?" I expand myself in a way that connects with my inner peace and repeat the simple, benign, purely mental request. I want to emphasize there is no body language or other suggestive movement on my part.

Moments later, the lady puts down her book, reaches for an unopened package of pretzels, opens it up, and offers me one in the most polite way. Coincidence? Perhaps. However, if I told you that I have experienced this same outcome many hundreds of times in a vast multitude of different circumstances, would it then validate that something powerful is at work?

Think of yourself as a radio station. If you are emitting love and peace, it seems that people perceive this and receive your emissions of love and peace. Similarly, if you are emitting negativity in any form, people will also receive this signal from your personal radio station and you will receive signals of negativity. You need to decide what you want to emit. Now, if you do emit love and inner peace, you will find that you have tapped into the "power grid of life." It exists. It connects all of us. It is the source of unexplained miracles. It is the power that fuels acts of unselfishness and goodwill. It is the thrilling feeling you have inside when you know you have done something good for another human being. It is the feeling you get when you connect with the beauty of nature when you are on a hike or sitting by the beach. You are connected to all things through the power grid of life.

Why be connected? I am not advocating that you use your connectedness to pull off third-rate magic tricks like getting pretzels on plane trips. Kidding aside, once connected, you can experience *everything* in a fuller way. You are not blocked by the cinder block wall of ego. You see nature in all its true beauty. You see others for all of their truly beautiful inner qualities. You are an open radio station to receive the omnipresent power and love that exists in the universe and are free to transmit on that same grid. It is the most wonderful feeling, and you actually feel not only separated from ego but additionally feel as if your physical self can traverse the vast power grid of the universe. You can "fly" in a manner of speaking. You are one with the universe, and the universe lives inside of you.

Right at this moment, you are pure energy. We all are by the basic principles of physics. We are made up of molecules that in turn are made up of atoms that contain particles connected by the energy of the universe. Most of us learn that all matter, including your body, is 99.9 percent empty space. If I were to use Yankee Stadium to model of a single atom, the nucleus of that atom would be smaller than the size of a baseball placed on the pitcher's mound (about three times smaller to provide you some sense of scale). The electrons are even smaller and orbit the nucleus at energy levels that are either "higher" or "lower" based upon the energy of the atom (envision a small particle traveling around and around the stadium-model ether in the outer seats or within the field with greater and smaller radial distance from the ball on the pitcher's mound). Higher energy would translate to electrons at higher orbits and far faster vibration for the atom. The inverse is true for atoms that contain low energy. The electrons drop to lower orbits and "light" exits the atom. These are facts of physics.

You, and every single thing in the universe, are made of the very same cosmic dust built upon atoms. I submit to you this: because you are energy, you can connect to the universe of energy around you. Your mind and true self (or what some might call the soul) enable you to actually put yourself at a higher energy level. This is something we can feel. While it is difficult to describe, when you are living your true self and feel genuine joy, there is an energy you can feel both in the mind and the body. This is when you know you are connecting to God or the power of the universe. This is the state in which your body and mind naturally want to reside.

Now, it is your responsibility to tap into the power of the universe. Emit positivity from your personal radio station. Find your true inner self, follow that path, and find that your mind and body will be closely connected to the power of the universe for all your days going forward.

~ Personal Notes ~

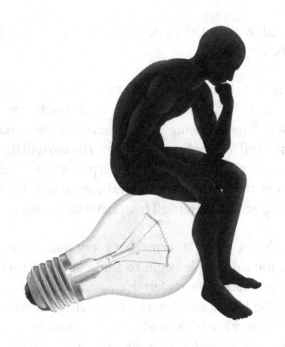

Meditation: Finding Your True Inner Self and Destiny

At this point, you are likely rather skeptical. I can understand. All of this "power of the universe" stuff seems a bit nebulous. Well, in fact, it is. The only way to tap into the power of the universe is to find your own true inner self. You need to uncover the God-given gifts that were bestowed upon you and the universe around you wants or even demands, that these wonderful gifts are released to make the world around you a more positive and better place.

Herein lies the big question; how to I uncover my true inner self? First, you need to fully acknowledge that the ego will fight to ensure you continue to believe you are all the "stuff" you built up over time. The ego will fight to ensure you remain disconnected and purely an individual. It is a matter of the ego's survival within you. The best way to disconnect yourself from ego is to meditate.

Now, do not panic. It seems that every time meditation is mentioned, people begin to think about sitting the floor, in a rather uncomfortable position, and moaning unintelligible phrases. No. This is not what I am referring to in the very least. You will not be required to stand on one leg and raise the other above your head with your eyes closed.

The type of meditation I am talking about is completely natural, and it is as necessary for cleansing your inner self as brushing your teeth is for proper oral hygiene. Let's take a simple case. Let's say you have a thirty-minute commute to work. Disconnect from your cell phone, music, or anything that would block nearly complete silence. Then do some true introspection. Look inside yourself. Are you happy? If you are not happy, think of times when you were. What was it about those moment of happiness that gave you joy? Why do you or don't you like about your job? What would you rather be doing with your life? Who, of the people you know, do you wish you were closer to? Why? What things excite you and strongly motivate you?

This is something you are going to have to do quite a bit of. Meditation is the lone path to finding your true inner self.

Here is another suggestion. Sit in your most comfortable chair and look out of the window at nature. Be sure that you are in a quiet environment as best as can be managed. I strongly suggest in these moments that you use a simple technique when starting to meditate, which involves closing your eyes when possible, breathing deeply in through your nose, holding that very deep breath momentarily, and then as slowly as possible, breathing out through pursed lips as if you're filling an imaginary balloon with all your inner stress. This simple technique, performed for about five to ten times at the start of meditation, will take your mind off the events swirling around you and put you completely in the present moment. Now you can begin to expose your true inner self, and you begin to look inside at the emotions you feel during these moments. At this point, perform the question and answer introspection pattern I describe above. Write down what you are feeling. Document those things that seem to hit precisely the right spot, the things that make you happy. Do not prejudge what you find— even if it at first it seems absurd. When you begin to feel that you are finding your true inner self, you are going to feel your inner energy jump. You will feel this elevated energy in your mind and body. Let these feelings be your compass. They will guide you, as you document over time, to who you are truly meant to be.

Brace yourself. You are very likely to find, after repeated meditation, that things in your life are quite misaligned and that you are currently on the wrong path for your true inner self. You may live in a city apartment, but remember the total sense of joy you had on your grandfather's horse farm in the country. You may find that family life was never what you intended, but rather, your true inner self points you toward a freer lifestyle. Perhaps you are an engineer and all you really want to do is teach and help others by sharing your skills. The field of possibilities is endless, but you will arrive, after repeated meditation, with a strong sense of the direction your life *must* take. I say *must* because your true inner self cannot lie to you. It is what you genuinely are. Nothing can change that. Your universe-given gifts will explode in your inner mind, and your energy level will go through the roof. You will encounter so much energy once you define your inner gifts that you will find the need to jump out of your chair and begin pursuing them immediately.

You are already thinking about the downside of following the path of your inner gifts. Of course you are. "Well, I would really like to write, but I need to earn a living to feed my family." "I can't teach because it would require I go back to school for certifications, and even when I am done, my income will be cut in half." "I can't divorce my spouse despite my true inner feelings because we have two children." These statements are not meant to be quips. These are very real consequences of uncovering the life your inner self needs you to be. I wish I had a magic wand and could make very real life obstacles disappear on your path to your true and most sincere self. I can say, however, that if you analyze the "can't" statements that your mind forms, you will find that there is a lot of "ego" in there that wants desperately to save itself.

"You can't be a writer because you will no longer be able to make big bucks doing X, Y, and Z." This is what your disconnected, ever-hungry ego needs you to keep saying to yourself.

"You cannot leave your city apartment behind for a simpler life in the country because of what all your friends will say." Here again, ego wants you to maintain your false façade built up for your network of friends and family.

While it will not remove all obstacles and challenges, I can say with full confidence that if you work to strip any measure of ego from your "can't" statements, the path to your joyful, inner self will look far easier. You will no longer care what your parents, colleagues, or others say. You will not care about changes in income. You will, rather, only care that you are going to put yourself on the path to inner joy. That requires that you break down the cinder block wall of ego and confidently move in the direction of your given talents, gifts, and self-truth.

All of this requires a leap of faith—faith in deciding for yourself what your true path needs to be. This is not recklessness or selfishness in the least. Rather, the universe designed you *specifically* to use your inner gifts to make the world a better place. It will not look like it from the start, but concerns about income, status, relationships with others, and so forth, that may be holding you back, will fade if you place your full vigor into accomplishing the destiny meant for you given your particular gifts. You will know a peace and a true sense of success that few people ever know. It's your responsibility to yourself and to the world around you to follow your natural path in life.

If you feel a bit lost about tapping into your true self, it is completely natural. Remember, years have gone by that have established a fixed image of yourself born from your ego. I recommend you take time to answer these questions. Write down your replies. This will help you organize your thoughts, and as a result, your inner compass will be on a "better setting" when you meditate:

1) *If you knew it was impossible to fail, what would you do with your life?*
2) *If have won the lottery tomorrow, what activities would you focus on?*
3) *What in life are you completely passionate about? What topics stimulate your core beliefs?*
4) *During what activities do you find yourself experiencing effortless flow and a complete loss of awareness regarding the passage of time?*
5) *What makes you happiest in your life? Can you recall those moments in your life when you were the happiest?*
6) *What skill or ability do you display that draws others to spontaneously ask you for help or thank you for?*
7) *What do you consider to be your most precious talents and gifts? Could these be put to use to make the world around you a better place? How?*

8) *What people completely inspire you to the depths of your soul? Why?*

9) *If you shed all feeling of potential judgment and envisioned yourself "completely starting over," what would you choose to do with your life? Where? Why?*

10) *At the end of your days, what would you want others to remember you as being? How do you want your life remembered, revered, and what in your view will leave a positive, lasting legacy?*

Think through these carefully. This is not meant to be an easy set of questions nor should they be answered without the required deep introspection. Take time to develop thoughtful answers. As you think about the answers, chase away ego. Ego will relentlessly move you toward discomfort as you consider anything outside the status quo. You have but one life, and the status quo is not what God intended for you. Rather, the power of the universe wants you to feel totally passionate about life, totally inspired in each moment, and totally in alignment with your deepest inner beliefs. It is then, and only then, that you will be on the proper path specifically meant for you.

~ Personal Notes ~

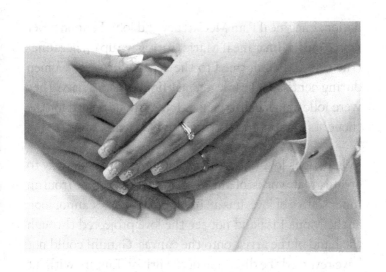

All You Need is Love

"All you need is love; love is all you need" - The Beatles

Consider what you have read so far. Once you remove ego out of your personal equation, you gain clarity. This clarity takes the shape of the universe, telling your inner self to travel the path you were meant to travel. In fact, the universe will align to enable you to begin using the personal gifts. Using your gifts makes you a better person and creates a better place for those around you. In a larger sense, you will be making the world a better place. Imagine if Michelangelo never sculpted. Imagine if Itzhak Perlman never played the violin. Imagine if Gandhi never applied the concepts of nonviolence to free a nation. Imagine if Paul McCartney and John Lennon never wrote music. Imagine if Marie Curie gave up on her inner true self and conformed to the accepted role of women during her time. These legendary figures had clarity. They were following their true passion without regard for the thoughts and potential criticisms of others.

Where does love enter this equation? There is no way to create great works, of any kind, unless they come from an inner source of love. It is an impossibility. One cannot look at the Mona Lisa and not see the love projected through the hand of the artist onto the canvas. Gandhi could not have reversed the direction of the British Empire without a beaming inner love that overcame the most incredible odds. These individuals were projecting, on the proper inner energy frequency for them that enabled their gifts to be shared with the world. This was their personal message to be transmitted on their radio station as it were. And, the power to transmit came from a place of love.

Let's approach this from the other side. If you do not love who you are, you can never find inner peace. This is a fact of life. We all know it to be true. That said, we must be cautious when we go through the looking glass from the other side. Self-love might mean that ego is back in play: "I love my big house." "I love my Maserati."

No. This is not what I mean by loving yourself. You will only know that you truly love yourself when you are doing those things that align with your universe or God-given gifts. You can only hear and understand what these are when you place yourself in a state of inner quiet, through the practice of meditation, and hear the truth being told to you. You will feel the meaninglessness of other "things." Said differently, you will experience the lack of love for those things in your life that do not align with you. These are things that take you off the path you were meant to travel.

It begins with love. You must feel and project love in every way possible, and this is only possible when you love the direction you are following in your life. You have found alignment with your gifts. You are aligned with your passion. Now, your inner light of love shines for the entire world to see and experience.

~ Personal Notes ~

I Am That I Am

I always found the biblical story of Exodus—the story of Moses and the freeing of the Israelites—to be rather interesting. I have no proof that specific events described in Exodus actually occurred, such as the miraculous parting of the Red Sea. However, someone took the time to document these events, and it shows up in the Old Testament of the Bible.

As a child, I was always taken with the 1956 movie version of *The Ten Commandments*. If you are a millennial or are part of Generation X, perhaps you have never seen this old classic. It was a grand spectacle of a movie directed by the great Cecil B. DeMille, and the lead role of Moses was portrayed by the legendary actor, Charlton Heston. But I digress. The whole story of Exodus seems to make sense except for one part: "I am that I am."

It will benefit us to recap the story of Exodus. We have the story of a Jewish infant that was placed in a basket and floated down the Nile River in Egypt so as to escape decreed execution of all Hebrew boys, and perhaps by chance, experience a better life than the one in store for any child in slavery. The infant child is found in the floating basket by an Egyptian princess and he, Moses, is adopted and raised as an Egyptian prince. Through a series of unforeseen events, it is discovered at the time of his adulthood that Moses is the offspring of Hebrew slaves. He is deemed to have committed high treason against Pharaoh and is banished from Egypt. His punishment is to walk through a seemly unending desert that would assure his demise. Against all odds, Moses survives his trek through the desert, albeit barely, and sees the light. By this, I mean he sees that God had saved him to carry out the specific purpose God intended for him.

So far, the story of Exodus seems like a well-written novel. It could all just be a very good story and completely fictional. The plot and action of the story are very compelling indeed. A slave child, turned Egyptian prince, turned outcast, now hears the word of God. It all works. The storyline is as good as any novel you may read in modern times and perhaps better. Then, something happens to Moses, as many of you may be aware. He climbs to the top of Mt. Sinai and sees a burning bush and hears the voice of God. Moses' first question is perhaps a simple, yet relevant one. "What is your name?" As is written in the book of Exodus, God responds, "I Am That I Am."

Now, this is what always struck me as odd. Let's say all of Exodus was just a good ol', fictional yarn written down by our highly imaginative and creative ancestors. If this were the case, right at the climactic moment when Moses speaks to God, our storywriter comes up with a name for God that is "I Am That I Am." What? It seems to me, if this was simply just good storytelling and fiction, the writer could have come up with something far better and more concrete. Perhaps a traditional Jewish name like "Jacob" would have suited. Perhaps a name such as "I Am the Beginning and the End." Perhaps something simple and omnipotent such as "The One" would have worked well. But no. Exodus documents that God reveals to Moses that his name is "I Am That I Am."

The fact that "I Am That I Am" is documented in the story of Exodus makes the story that much more believable, at least for me. It seems out of place with someone who is trying to create the fictional story of an all-powerful, all-caring, all-knowing God. The choice of words is too out of place to be made up. Yet, upon closer inspection, the words "I Am that I Am" seem to tie together with the fact that God made man in his own image. If this is the case, God, and by extension man, is what he is.

For our purposes here, we need to recognize that we are, each of us, what we were made by the universe to be. We are what we are. Nothing can change that. Man is a reflection of God himself, and should you believe in God, is what he is. He is born and has a specific makeup. His abilities will reflect what he truly is.

Now, for those who do not believe in God as a higher power, I completely respect your view of the world. That said, science does tell us that each human has a double-helix genetic code in the form of DNA that is the specific "blueprint" for that specific human being. If I were able to remove the DNA from a person and attempt to create a clone using the very same strands of DNA, the outcome would be exactly the same being. This is scientific fact and it is indisputable. The physical attributes of the "original" person and the predispositions or "talents" of the theoretical clone would be the same. It is no different than eye color, hair color, height, predisposition to disease, foot size, hand size, and on and on.

So believers and nonbelievers can agree that there is a power that organizes the universe, whether divine or not, that make us who and what we are. In short, we are what we are. And, it is that place that we need to get to. This is, by definition, our beginning and must be our destination. It is our "destiny," in other words, to fulfill gifts provided with our very given nature. From birth, we are imprinted with gifts from the universe that somehow conspire to make us who we are. The true way to live the peaceful path in life is to live in complete alignment with that design and that destiny.

It will provide clarity for you to repeat in quiet moments of meditation that "I Am That I Am." You are what you are. No pursuit of wealth, or fame, or other worldly objects, can change that. You may try to modify the universe's design that was created for you, but you will find yourself

34

out of alignment. I submit that you will find misalignment equivalent to a deep feeling of emptiness and isolation. You will no longer be connected to your purpose nor the power of the universe. Bluntly stated, you will be living a lie, the lie created by the ego and the many cinder blocks your ego has stacked over a lifetime. It is up to you to recognize that you are what you are. Be still and quiet. Connect with your innermost and true self. Discover your true purpose and align your life with your given gifts. This is the only path to true peace and genuine happiness.

~ Personal Notes ~

Good Vibrations

"I'm pickin' up good vibrations" – The Beach Boys

Earlier, I mentioned that it is important for you to view yourself as a kind of radio station. If you're emitting love, you should receive love. If you're emitting peace, you should be at peace. Through my own personal experience (remember the pretzels), I have seen that people can pick up your vibrations. This is nonverbal and nonphysical communication between people. Once you strip yourself of ego and connect with the power of the universe, you find your true self. In finding your true self, you find love. The inner joy this experience brings is unbelievably uplifting and your "good vibrations" will be picked up by those around you. Moreso, the universe will begin to align events such that they are in sync with the vibrations you are emitting. Yes, I am stating that once you find your particular frequency and are emitting it, the power of the universe will work in your favor. Events will occur that align with your given purpose and you will arrive and at your natural destination or achieve your destiny. This will occur for you and by design the universe will ensure it shall be so.

I have seen the force of good vibrations manifest itself in my life. Have you ever been thinking about an old friend and suddenly you run into them or they call you unexpectedly? Have you ever been thinking about accomplishing something and you find that you are at dinner with someone who is the perfect fit for you to achieve the outcome you have been thinking about? Have you ever envisioned a perfect outcome and events proceed exactly as you dreamed? The answer is yes, a thousand times yes. If you emit positive vibrations, things will show up, rather unexpectedly, in your life to help get you to your destiny. Put another way, the universe naturally wants you to be able to share your God-given gifts and therefore, will align events to best enable you to share them with the world.

The flip side of good vibrations is "worry." The human race has wasted more energy on the practice of worry than on any other single thing over the course of history. The result has been nothing. Worrying about something is nonaction of the most egregious kind. Yet we all do it ... yes? We lay down to sleep and we worry about the business trip we are going to take the next day. We worry about getting ill. We worry about money. We worry about the future. Guess what? All the worrying in the world will never change the outcome. The energy poured into worry is poured down the drain. It is a sad but very real part of the human condition.

I do not mean to make light of worry. Worry drives the human mind toward depression. Worry can tragically drive us toward suicide. We find ourselves taking medication to avoid the consequences of worry in the form of depression.

Worry's close friend is "stress." Stress is the physical and mental manifestation of the practice of worrying. We live in modern times, and we see that we all face greater stress. Worse yet, when we actually accomplish something we have been worried about, we now think to ourselves, "OK, now I have to do something great once again." Here, ego is at work, wanting more and more. Stress actually increases as opposed to decreasing. Ego will protect the cinder block wall you created and force you to worry and worry and worry some more about bigger and better accomplishments.

The only escape from worry is to strip yourself of ego and connect with your true inner self. Why does this work? If you put yourself on the path that you were destined to be on, the path that gives your life joy and meaning, there is no worry. You know that the universe will conspire, because of your "good vibrations," to ensure you arrive at your determined destiny. There is no longer the problem of worry. You have inverted worry into the power of emitting positive thoughts from your own radio station. Those emissions will be picked up by people in your life, and the world around you will help get you to your destination. You will find yourself approaching the place where your God-given gifts can be put to work and make the world a better place. All worry is at an end. Perhaps the world's best documented quote regarding worry came from Jesus, as written by Matthew: "Therefore I tell you, do not worry about your life, what you will eat or drink; or about your body, what you will wear. Is not life more than food, and the body more than clothes? Look at the birds of the air; they do not sow or reap or store away in barns, and yet your heavenly Father feeds them. Are you not much more valuable than they? Can any one of you by worrying add a single hour to your life?" (Matthew 6:25).

Good vibrations will get you there.

Good vibrations do not only eliminate worry, but they can invert the negative energy associated with many human emotions. If you emit love toward a person that has wronged you, you will note that you no longer feel emotional injury. You will very likely find that people will "come around" and actually change their negative opinion. In quite a different realm, if you are suffering from a disease or addiction and you apply the principles of good vibrations toward the inner disturbance within you, you will find, quite often, that you pain and suffering will ease.

It is your radio station. What vibrations do you choose to emit? What vibrations do you wish others to receive? What vibrations do you want to have a positive impact on your own personal health? It is your choice.

~ Personal Notes ~

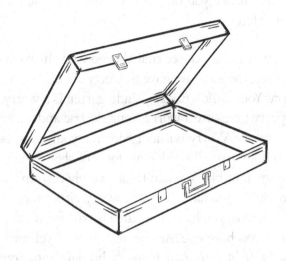

Less Is More

Perhaps you own a home. That means you likely have homeowner's insurance because you are worried about something happening to your home. You cut the grass or tend to your property. You paint the home to ensure it looks acceptable to other people, as you need to keep your standard aligned with the opinions others have. You may pay for a maid to clean your home for similar reasons. You find that you need to fill a room with the proper furniture, and this causes you to take out a loan. Now, you need new curtains and flooring. You and your spouse decide you need to redo the bathroom, and this will be a significant expense, hence you take out a home equity loan. More. More. More.

By now it is easy to see that the more "stuff" we have in our lives, the more we have to worry about. Your car is a worry. Your child's private kindergarten is a worry. Your property taxes are a worry. Your electric and water bills are a worry. Worry without end. Yet, your home is your shelter, and we all need some form of shelter no matter how small or big. You can be absolutely certain that the more things you have, the more worry, either conscious or unconscious, you have. The same is true for your spouse, should you have one. At the most basic level, each new item brought into your home or brought into your life, no matter how insignificant, is actually adding to your overall field of worry.

Perhaps you need proof. Why is it that so many of us do some form of "spring cleaning"? We rid ourselves of unwanted things, and, low-and-behold, we feel great after purging ourselves of "stuff."

I personally experienced this during one of my numerous moves. I was attempting to throw out old Christmas ornaments that I had them stacked in a Rubbermaid bin. Yes, each ornament had some special memory. I made two piles: one for the "keepers" and one the "rubbish." After the first go through, there were far too many keepers. A second pass through the items increased the rubbish pile. I experienced a very real, physical sensation as I moved each individual item from the keeper pile to the rubbish pile. I was feeling increased relief. It was actually joyful to rid myself of so many truly unnecessary objects. Eventually, I got to the point where I kept literally two or three items that really had very specific and special meaning to me. Now the rubbish pile had hundreds of little, meaningless objects and I could not have been happier when they were tossed.

Many of you will note that older apartments or homes have far smaller closets then new construction. Why? People used to live with far less stuff. Modern living means living with lots of stuff: holding on to cell phone charging cords used for a phone you had ten years ago, the pants that you wore in 1995, an old sports jersey that no longer fits but you had during one particular game. *Rubbish.*

Rid your life of this extra stuff. With each item you toss (and let me be clear, I strongly recommend you donate to charity as much as possible in this process), you will reduce your stress and worry. By ridding yourself of worry, you are placing yourself closer to inner peace and your true inner purpose and destiny.

In your quiet moments of meditation, ask yourself if you could live if you got rid of X, Y, or Z. You are going to find that you really need very few things, and you will rid your life of much unneeded worry. Moreover, you will increase your inner joy and increase your ability to output good vibrations. Yes, less is more. Keep less in your life, and you will be happier for it.

~ Personal Notes ~

How Can I Serve?

The power of the universe is accessible when ego is removed. Ego prevents connectedness and is counter to our efforts to manifest our true inner selves and arrive at our true destiny. The question now becomes this: how can the process of self-actualization, in the form of accessing your gifts and achieving your true destiny, be accelerated? Meditation is certainly one path. You need to keep yourself centered and away from egocentric thinking. Quiet time for you to do introspection will help this process immensely. There is one other way that will put you on a fast track toward your destiny, and that is serving your fellow man.

I was fortunate enough, recently, to be able to help a family friend. In the past, if this person had asked for the kind of help they were seeking, I would not have been "present" enough in the moment to truly provide any help. This time, however, I decided that I was going to do every possible thing in my power to genuinely help this person, without any expectation of anything in return. Zero. I would simply put my full and best efforts to ensure this person got everything being asked of me. The result was astounding for the person I was helping. Without outlining the details, the situation this family friend was in completely turned around and became a total success story. No one could have scripted a better outcome. When all was said and done, the family friend was absolutely overjoyed. Of course, I was showered with thank yous. But, I was mentally sure to align myself with the fact that I had no other expectations in return.

Two things did occur as a result of this unselfish act of love. First, I personally felt terrific. I cannot describe the personal happiness I derived simply by ensuring the best possible outcome for a friend. I felt connected to this friend, and my connectedness seemed to transcend my relationship with this person. Second, rather unexpectedly, something wonderful emerged in my life in the form of an unexpected opportunity. Prior to my helping this family friend, the likelihood of this particular opportunity showing up in my life was near zero. Now, coincidently, at the time I help another human being without expectation of payback, the power of the universe seem to present me with a gift. Coincidence?

Perhaps. I can tell you, however, that my own personal feeling of joy alone was worth all of the efforts put into the help provided. Hence, I knew my radio station was on a "high-power," good vibration level. It seems inevitable that something good was destined to come back my way.

My simple advice is to help others completely and unselfishly. The "unselfish" part is the key. If, in the back of your mind, you really expect the power of the universe to pay you back, the whole works will come tumbling down. You have to be honest and true within yourself when you are helping someone in need. If you do so in a genuine fashion, you can expect good things to come into your life that were previously unexpected. Help others if for no other reason than to bring love into the world and to bring joy to others. Then sit back and watch what happens.

~ Personal Notes ~

50

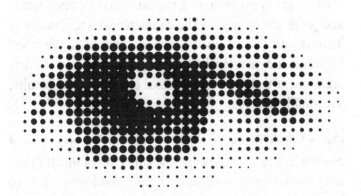

Look at Yourself, and Watch What Happens

As you begin to shift from being a person who is egocentric to one who is self-aware, valuable direction can be derived by "looking at yourself." What do I mean by "looking at yourself? Form a mental image of yourself stepping out of your own physical body and watching yourself in your day-to-day activities. What I am suggesting is that you become your own "audience" to your life. This simple technique has power beyond comprehension.

Why become your own audience? First, this is something that should be rather natural. We love to watch television or movies and watch characters on screen. When we watch a given performance, we can stand independently and judge the actions of the character we are observing. This is our goal when we look at ourselves. We want to stand independently and judge ourselves with any attachment to how events unfold or to the final results. We simply observe.

Oscar Wilde famously said, "To become the spectator of one's own life ... is to escape the suffering of life. It offers the key to the end of all suffering. All you have to do is to become a spectator of your own life." Wilde's observation is true of not only suffering but also all emotions. We observe ourselves and disconnect from being the individual involved. We can therefore judge more fairly and reasonably our actions. We can also separate from painful emotion. We also can see for ourselves whether we like the person we observe or not. Finally, we can determine, without emotion, if we want the person we see to be different.

Look at yourself and watch what happens. You will begin to look at your life and your actions from a totally different perspective, and that will make all the difference.

~ Personal Notes ~

53

Smile, Look, and Listen

In a life devoid of ego, you are pursuing your true inner gifts. You are connected with the world around you and, unmistakably, your life is filled with higher energy and love. It is important to understand that we are human and it is will be a life-long struggle to fight off ego and place yourself on the path for which you are destined. None of this will be simple, and you will need to continue to push yourself, using the techniques outlined, to stay the course. Integrating three elements into your everyday routine will help immensely: smiling, looking, and listening.

There have been numerous physiological studies about smiling. The first key fact is that smiling immediately stimulates parts of your brain associated with joy. Right now, while reading this book, put on a smile. You will immediately notice that it is impossible to smile without raising your inner sense of happiness. That is a rather power tool. Now, I must emphasize that your smile needs to be generated from "genuineness." People around you can readily tell if you are putting on a "plastic" or insincere smile. Think of something that brings you true joy and then smile. Your personal radio station will transmit thoughts of joy, and those who see you smiling will not be able to help but smile back. We see every day that smiling is contagious. We can brighten someone else's day by simply smiling at them. Moreover, we put our own state of mind in a place of inner joy.

Our minds race with the activities and stresses of the day. As a result, we find ourselves never "present" in the moment. You can be standing in the lobby of a beautiful hotel and not notice its beauty because your mind and ego are occupied with thoughts such as, "What room am I going to get?" or "What's the first thing I need to do after checking in?" It is a sad fact that most of us will spend nearly our entire life never fully experiencing a single moment because the ego has been left in the driver's seat, forcing you to think about what's next.

Try to calm your mind. Stop for a second when you are in the moment. Look at the beauty that surrounds us every day. Look into a child's eyes. Look at interesting architecture that may surround you. Look at the simply beauty of a flower or tree. Truly look at the beauty of the beach and the ocean. Stop your mind and halt the ego for enough time for you to deeply absorb all the beauty and power the universe has placed around us to enjoy. Doing so will raise your personal energy level and increase your inner joy immensely.

Listening is a critical life skill. Your ego wants you to chatter on about yourself, your problems, gossip, complain about the long line you are waiting on, fuss over the wait for a car or train, and endlessly on. It is far past time for you to listen. Yes, this means listening to others who will very likely be in their ego state. But be devoid of judgment and seek to fully listen to them and understand what they wish to communicate. Listen without interruption or insertion of advice or the inevitable finishing of the other person's sentences. Truly listen. Look into the eyes of a person talking to you and comprehend their situation, their inner pain, and their plight. Chances are that they will find that through your quiet, peaceful listening, they will see that you genuinely care. Here again, you must be sincere when listening to others. Be present in the moment. Think, while carefully listening, about how you may serve or help this person. Listen for cues that the power of the universe may be giving you about how this person may have come into your life to help you on the path to your true destiny. Think about how you might be able to relieve the burden of another person even by some small measure. Listening, in a true and genuine fashion, is very simply an act of immense kindness and love. As a result, you are placing yourself in the higher energy state that will radiate from you and provide you with inner peace.

~ Personal Notes ~

Surrendering: Trusting the Power of the Universe

We have established that striping away ego and proper meditation about your inner purpose will connect you to the power of the universe. Ralph Waldo Emerson stated, "The only person you are destined to become is the person you decide to be." Emerson also said, "Once you make a decision, the universe conspires to make it happen." In other words, once you established that you are moving toward the goals meant for you, you have the infinite power of the universe with you to ensure that your personal gifts are shared with the world.

So, all this is going to be easy, right? Not so fast. You will encounter difficulties, problems, and obstacles on your journey. Here is where your faith in powers greater is key. You have to be aware and awake to the help that will come your way. "Trust in the Lord with all your heart, and do not lean on your own understanding. In all your ways acknowledge him, and he will make straight your paths" (Proverbs 3:5-6). Here, the Bible tells us that powers greater than us will be there to help you.

Put your mind to your goals and work earnestly to make them happen. Then, as obstacles are encountered, meditate and ask the power of the universe for help. Surrender your problems to this higher power because you know it is aligning events, as it absolutely must, to ensure you achieve your inner purpose.

Lao Tzu taught us, "Yield and overcome ... empty and be full ... have little and gain ... The sage embraces the One." This quote is 2,500 years old, from the highly revered Chinese philosopher, Lao Tzu, and he understood what the philosophical giants of the bible through modern day philosophers, such as Emerson and Thoreau, understood as well. That once you are in alignment with your true purpose, the wind of the universe is at your back.

Some may be skeptical of the concept of surrendering your problems to a higher power. It is important to understand that the concept of surrendering is a spiritual action and displays trust in the inner guidance that you have been given. It does not mean "give up." Does a sailing ship at sea "give up" when it raises its sails to harness the power of the wind? Of course it does not. Rather, the captain and crew know that harnessing the power of the naturally occurring wind will move them along on their journey. This is the type of surrender I suggest here. Moreover, it is important to "ask" for such help.

Returning to our analogy, a captain needs to ask or command his crew to raise its sails. There is purpose in this action. Similarly, you need to ask the power of the universe, with a sense of purpose, for the help you need. Ask for help in quiet moments of meditation. Ask for strength, and strength will be given to you. Through surrendering, you allow the powers of the universe to help you on your journey. "Ask, and you shall receive!" (Matthew 7:7).

~ Personal Notes ~

Dealing With Crisis

Some of you may have come to this part of the book holding a fair amount of skepticism. I get it. You need to live out these principles to see how they may have an impact on your life. Worse, I know that a subset of you are dealing right now with true crisis in your life. Perhaps a family member is dying or has died. Perhaps you are suffering from a chronic or fatal disease. You may be dealing with significant financial pressures because of the loss of a job. Sadly, we need to accept that part of the human condition is suffering. As the saying goes, "Into each life, some rain shall fall." We just don't know when or in what form it will come. However, it will occur for you and for me, and it will sadly occur numerous times. While I pray and wish that the suffering in your life is kept at the absolute minimum, I know that you will at some point have to face hard times. If you are facing such a situation at the moment, you have my deepest and most sincere sympathies.

My advice is to apply the principles outlined herein:

1) Strip Away Ego

Why? If you lost a job, you need to separate the view that you are what you do from your true inner self. Losing your job may, in fact, provide an opportunity for you to align with your true self and your destiny. This may be the event that allows you to tap into and release your inner gifts.

2) Connect to the Power of the Universe

Why? Because once you are aligned to your true inner self, it brings peace to you and connectedness with the world around you. This will ease the pain and suffering that may occur when you lose a loved one, for example. I submit that while your loved one has left this physical world, their energy, or some may call it their spirit, is accessible through the power of the universe.

3) All you need is love

Use love to invert negativity that enters your life. If someone did you harm, send love back in that person's direction. Yes, this is very difficult, especially if the harm perpetrated left a deep, emotional wound in your life. You have a choice. You can perpetuate hate for the other person, which will dramatically have an impact on your ability to feel any sense of inner joy going forward. Or, you can radiate love, and the universe will have your back. The power of the universe will conspire to ensure that your emotional pain is eased

4) I Am That I Am

Give yourself a break, so to speak. You are what you are. If your source of crisis is due to your own failing, so be it. Accept yourself with all your gifts and all your faults. We are human, and by construction, we are not perfect. Let me break the news to you now: unless you have built the most massive cinder-block-ego wall the world has ever known, you know you are not perfect. That's the way it is. Accept it. Moreover, embrace your shortcomings. The crisis you face is very likely a sign that you are not aligned with your true inner gifts and destiny.

5) Good Vibrations

It's your radio station. What will you be emitting at times of crisis? Will it help if you are emitting vibrations of panic, despair, or worry? No. Remember that no amount of worry ever carried out by any human being that has ever lived has resulted in anything at all. Worry is worthless. The better path to follow is to get your radio station powered up to emit the highest form of positive vibrations. Your personal radio station will receive positivity in return.

6) Less Is More

Perhaps your crisis is divorce. This is an incredibly painful emotional situation. Beyond the techniques described above, you should use this sad event to rid your life of things you do not need. Make your life simpler in the process. Have fewer things, and feel the inner result of reduced stress. Despite the emotional pain, you will be getting back on a path to inner peace by ridding yourself of unnecessary "stuff."

7) How Can I Serve?

If you are suffering from a chronic or even fatal condition, get involved. Help others suffering from the same condition. Why? It will help you deal with your own personal crisis, and by helping others, in a totally unselfish manner, the power of the universe will conspire to ease your own suffering.

The same holds true for the crisis of illness in or death of a loved one, which we sadly all have to experience in our lifetime. I am not seeking to minimize the feeling of tremendous loss and despair experienced when someone we love dies or is suffering, but we have to acknowledge that our life continues.

The best way to pay homage to the loved one is to take up a cause. Perhaps that is caring for others who love the same person, involvement in disease charities, or helping others with a similar condition. Through our service, we will find a path to peace, as best as can be found, in the inevitable suffering of loved ones.

8) Look at Yourself, and Watch What Happens

Separate yourself from the situation by becoming purely an observer. Meditate on Oscar Wilde's quote, "To become the spectator of one's own life ... is to escape the suffering of life." It offers the key to the end of all suffering.

9) Smile, Look, and Listen

Tragic situations make it difficult to slow the racing mind. Instead, take the time to smile, look, and listen. If you are visiting a parent who is terminally ill, smile with them, look into their eyes, and genuinely listen. This may be your last and only chance to do so in a sincere way. Despite the tragic event of the passing of a loved one, you can make the inevitable a far better and loving situation simply by employing these simple steps.

We are all human, and we are destined to experience negative situations. It is up to you to determine how you will handle these situations. Despite the depth or seriousness of the problems you will face, you will enable yourself, and others around you, to be better able to deal with difficult moments with genuine smiling, looking, and listening.

10) Surrendering: Trusting the Power of the Universe

Know and trust that the power of the universe does not want you to suffer. "You do not have because you do not ask, ask and you shall receive!" (Matthew 7:7). This does not ensure that the crisis you are living through will be alleviated immediately or in the precise manner expected. Rather, your faith in a greater power and your sincerity in asking for help will manifest an easing of your suffering.

Personal crisis is real. The emotional scars are real. From the moment we are born, we need to understand that part of the human experience will be some form of suffering and crisis in our lives. There are no perfect solutions. I can only submit to you that putting the above principle into practice, when you find yourself in crisis, will help ease your pain.

~ Personal Notes ~

Doing No Harm

The power of the universe gave you specific gifts in order to make the world around you a better place. This, by definition, means that harm of any kind is not part of the path you will be on. When I say harm of any kind, I mean this: emotional harm you might be causing others, harm you might be doing to yourself by not eating properly or not getting enough sleep, harm you might unintentionally cause your partner by not helping out and being supportive of the other person's burden, harm that you may be doing to the earth, intentional or not, by overaccumulating things and thereby stripping the earth of natural resources. I also mean harm in the form of dislike or hate you may harbor for another individual.

Harm is an act of selfishness. You do harm to others when you solely seek to serve your own purpose and goals. This once again is the ego at work. The result can only poison you and the world around you.

If we truly strip ourselves of ego, it is impossible for us to do harm. With ego banished from your life, you become conscious of your connectedness with the people and the natural world around you. It is impossible in this enlightened state for you to cause harm once you have entered this state of mind. Only love is present. Good vibrations cannot lead to harm.

So, if the principles outlined here prevent us from committing harm, why have I even bothered to discuss the topic? This is because unseen harm occurs with excesses. These excesses can take to form of drinking, smoking, stress-driven eating, arguing with loved ones, and so forth. Driving a massive SUV that emits greenhouse gasses into the atmosphere and makes our planet a more diminished place and harms animal organisms dependent upon our environment is doing harm.

Be conscious of the harms that occur with excess. The path to inner peace must be one without excess. Jesus preached, "If you want to be perfect, go, sell your possessions and give to the poor, and you will have treasure in heaven. Then come, follow me." Given our analysis of harm, it is not hard to see why Jesus would have stated this. Think before excesses. Think before you may cause unintentional harm.

~ Personal Notes ~

Little Miracles

Let's recap. We follow the set of principles set forth here. We strip away ego. We tap into the power of the universe. We are, therefore, connected to others and the world around us. Love enters our lives. We hear our inner calling, and our true gifts become evident. We align our path in life with the God-given or universe-given gifts provided to us. The result of aligning our lives with our inner gifts is true inner peace. Our inner joy causes us to transmit positive vibrations from our personal radio station, and the universe answer back in kind. OK, good work. But you still have more work to do.

Now, it will be your responsibility and, in fact, your obligation to be observant. The power of the universe is not going to drop a baby grand piano into your living room simply because you tapped into the fact that one of our God-given gifts is music.

Allow me this hyperbole to make the point. The power of the universe will conspire to help you in subtle ways. It is your job to observe carefully and pick up when the universe is providing an opportunity for you to access and use the gifts, as it wants you to use to make the world a better place.

What does this mean? Perhaps you are sitting in a restaurant, and you feel a slight tingling in the pit of your stomach that signals that you should strike up a conversation with the person sitting at the table close to you. Go with your gut. These little feelings are directions coming from the universe. In our example, you decide to talk to this person. You may find out that this person has the precise skill set that will advance you on the path to achieve your true destiny. Once you have tapped into the power grid of the universe, you will find that events will suddenly begin to line up in your favor. However, you need to trust yourself.

Perhaps you have a powerful inner feeling that compels you to travel to Paris. You have no idea what the connection could be. However, it is clear that you keep feeling this push from the universe for you to travel to Paris. Trust your gut. Go to Paris. Something will happen in Paris that will place you on a more precise path toward using your gifts and achieving your destiny.

How will you know that your gut is telling you to do something to further you on your true path? I cannot answer that for you. I do know that I have had such feelings, and they have happened repeatedly.

I am not referring to acting on whims. These genuine feelings are far more than whims and can be characterized as repetitive little pushes that the universe is giving you to get you on the right path.

These are the little miracles. These are the things that happen out of the blue that conspire to expose your gifts. It is the unexpected phone call from an old friend. It is the unexpected check that arrives in the mail. It is the random person you meet on a plane who somehow helps you toward your goal. It is the book or poem that you randomly read that somehow provides special meaning for you. Even seemingly negative events, such as the loss of a job, can be the universe's way of directing you toward your true, aligned path. You need to be self-aware and sensitive to the little miracles that will be coming your way. Don't despair. If you miss a signal for some reason, the universe does not give up. Something else will come your way to get you aligned with your true path. Be alert. Connect with your true inner self. You will find little miracles coming into your life in bunches.

~ Personal Notes ~

Start with the End in Mind

It is likely you have read and heard much about "positive visualization." Athletes are often interviewed after winning something significant that they "visualized" themselves winning before the event occurred. We can all agree that visualization is very powerful, and, with regard to achieving the goals your inner self has defined, using visualization is a powerful and useful tool.

That said, there seems to be more to "visualization" than the simple act of your mind seeing itself in a given, desired end-state. Here again, I submit that the power of the universe will pick up the signals being transmitted from your personal radio station. If you are transmitting joy as a result of feeling positive as a result from a positive outcome, the universe will reply in kind. Note, your transmission has to come from a place that is devoid of ego and filled with love. Think of it in these terms. The universe is far more likely to support the athlete that wants to genuinely win for his teammates and for love of his family than the cocky athlete that trash talks that he will win.

There is the finest of lines between true inner confidence and egocentric overconfidence. What type of confidence you are feeling and transmitting at any given moment will depend on the inner energy and positivity that you sense within your mind and body. If you feel sincere "good vibrations," that would be a sure clue that your desires are coming from a state of love.

There is another aspect to visualization that I cannot fully explain. You will recall that we talked about the story of Exodus and God's proclamation of "I Am That I Am." There is true divine power in the statement, "I Am." If you tell yourself, in times of quiet, peaceful meditation, "I am healthy," you will generally manifest more health in your life. If you choose to focus on "I am loving," you will find that more love of all types will show up in your life. Why? Let's remember your inner radio station. The statement, "I Am," assumes the result is already achieved. This seems to significantly amplify the signal you are transmitting. By thinking about a situation with a positive conclusion already in mind, you are emitting the most powerful signal your personal radio station can emit.

Be mindful that the use of "I Am" and visualizing a positive outcome is not present in the power of the universe for you to win the lottery. Here again, allow me the use of hyperbole to make a point. What you ask of the universe must come from your true inner self, and, as we discussed, this is the domain of love. If your goal is to unselfishly help others and spread your God-given gifts to make the world a better place (much like talented and blessed athletes, writers, musicians, painters, entrepreneurs, volunteers, doctors, inventors, etc.), then the signals transmitted on your personal radio station will be heard, and the universe will conspire to help you achieve your goals.

~ Personal Notes ~

81

The Long and Winding Road: Getting on the Path to your Joyous Self

Shakespeare, in my humble view, understood the human condition better than anyone prior to him, and his works, to this day, still are able to express human qualities and shortcomings in a brilliant and captivating way.

Humans are what they are. They have been that way since separating from lower primates roughly 200,000 years ago. While the human race has accumulated great knowledge over that time, there is no evidence that we have evolved emotionally. Shakespeare understood the universal truths about human emotion and masterfully exposed them through his writing and plays.

Why should we pay homage to Shakespeare? If for no other reason at all, it is because he wrote the words, "This above all—to thine own self be true." These nine words summarize all that we should be. These nine words summarize all that we should strive for in our lives. These nine words, if heeded, will lead us directly toward exposing our God-given gifts and put us on course to our true destiny. One can make that case that, with regard to improving the joy that we experience in life, there are no more important words ever written. If you are true to yourself, everything else in your life will fall perfectly into place. You will never feel the need to compare yourself to others as the ego suggests. You will always feel inner peace because you are being true to your own gifts and talents. You will emit love because you will, by definition, be connected to the power of the universe.

If you read this book, it is because you feel some emptiness. Perhaps you felt a small, tingling sensation to get this book that you cannot describe. Whatever got you to this point, it is now up to you to put this method to work so that you can truly live the most joyous form of your life. It is time. Quiet your mind. Do the proper introspection. Reconnect with your true inner self. Then take the steps outlined.

You will have to make choices, and those choices will be difficult. Are you truly prepared to leave your current well-paying job because you feel you are most aligned and passionate when you envision yourself as a nurse, a teacher, a writer, or any one of a million other possibilities? This is up to you in the end.

Know that you would be far from alone in any quest you decide to undertake. History has proved that people with high passion demonstrate unshakable confidence in pursuit of their goals. Picasso, Maria Montessori, Albert Einstein, Mozart, Shakespeare, Tesla, Joseph Pulitzer, the Wright Brothers, Florence Nightingale, Gandhi, Steve Jobs, Nelson Mandela, Marie Curie, Abraham Lincoln, Richard Pryor, Galileo, Susan B. Anthony, Charlie Parker, Sigmund Freud, St. Francis of Assisi, Rosa Parks, Edgar Allan Poe, and hundreds upon thousands others all faced personal ruin, bankruptcy, and complete failure before their single-minded, passionate pursuit of their goals changed the world.

With the proper introspection, you will uncover your universe-provided gifts and talents. These will not be of the mediocre sort. These will be talents that will make the world a better place. It is your destiny. More so, the universe will line up to help you pour your special gifts into the world because *you were meant to do so.*

So my final advice is to be brave. To thine own self be true. Follow the long and winding road that gets you to fully align with your special gifts. Your reward will be a life unlike any you could have ever imagined, and one filled with infinite joy.

~ Personal Notes ~

Addendum: Important Life Quotes

I strongly recommend that you make the reading of positive philosophy, quotes, poetry, and other uplifting writing part of your meditation practice. Why? Quiet reading of uplifting writing may expose truths to you and place you on a more direct path toward inner peace and your destiny. I provide some interesting quotes here. I recommend that you seek out writing that you find to be specifically uplifting for you.

"Go confidently in the direction of your dreams! Live the life you've imagined."
—Henry David Thoreau

"May you live all the days of your life."
—Jonathan Swift

"Dost thou love life? Then do not squander time, for that is the stuff life is made of."
—Benjamin Franklin

"Life is either a daring adventure or nothing at all."
—Helen Keller

"Only a life lived for others is a life worthwhile."
—Albert Einstein

"Keep smiling, because life is a beautiful thing and there's so much to smile about."
—Marilyn Monroe

"When ego is lost, limit is lost. You become infinite, kind, beautiful."
—Yogi Bhajan

"You have brains in your head. You have feet in your shoes. You can steer yourself any direction you choose."
—Dr. Seuss

"And God said unto Moses, I Am That I Am."
—Exodus 3:14

"The only impossible journey is the one you never begin."
—Anthony Robbins

"Love the life you live. Live the life you love."
—Bob Marley

"Do not let making a living prevent you from making a life."
—John Wooden

"The purpose of our lives is to be happy."
—Dalai Lama

"Live in the sunshine, swim the sea, drink the wild air."
—Ralph Waldo Emerson

"The greatest pleasure of life is love."
—Euripides

"The energy of the mind is the essence of life."
—Aristotle

"Therefore I tell you, do not worry about your life, what you will eat or drink; or about your body, what you will wear. Is not life more than food, and the body more than clothes? Look at the birds of the air; they do not sow or reap or store away in barns, and yet your heavenly Father feeds them. Are you not much more valuable than they? Can any one of you by worrying add a single hour to your life?"
—Matthew 6:25

"Let us always meet each other with smile, for the smile is the beginning of love."
—Mother Teresa

"In the end, it's not the years in your life that count. It's the life in your years."
—Abraham Lincoln

"Change is the law of life, and those who look only to the past or present are certain to miss the future."
—John F. Kennedy

"To be yourself in a world that is constantly trying to make you something else is the greatest accomplishment."
—Ralph Waldo Emerson

"If one advances confidently in the direction of his dreams and endeavors to live the life which he has imagined, he will meet with a success unexpected in common hours."
—Henry David Thoreau

"Don't imagine that your perfection lies in accumulating or possessing external things. Your perfection is inside of you. If only you could realize that, you would not want to be rich. Ordinary riches can be stolen from a man. Real riches cannot. In the treasury-house of your soul, there are infinitely precious things that may not be taken from you. And so, try to so shape your life that external things will not harm you. And try also to get rid of personal property. It involves sordid preoccupation, endless industry, continual wrong. Personal property hinders Individualism at every step."
—Oscar Wilde

"Be empty of worrying.
Think of who created thought!
Why do you stay in prison
When the door is so wide open?"
—Rumi

"If you want to be perfect, go, sell your possessions and give to the poor, and you will have treasure in heaven. Then come, follow me."
—Matthew 19:21

"Give every man thine ear, but few thy voice."
—William Shakespeare; Hamlet Act I, Scene 3

"This above all—to thine own self be true,
And it must follow, as the night the day,
Thou canst not then be false to any man."
—William Shakespeare; Hamlet Act I, Scene 3

"To become the spectator of one's own life ... is to escape the suffering of life. It offers the key to the end of all suffering. All you have to do is to become a spectator of your own life."
—Oscar Wilde

"Once you make a decision, the universe conspires to make it happen."
—Ralph Waldo Emerson

"You do not have because you do not ask, ask and you shall receive!"
—Matthew 7:7

"Be melting snow.
Wash yourself of yourself."
—Rumi

"The only person you are destined to become is the person
you decide to be."
—Ralph Waldo Emerson

"When first I was put into prison, some people advised
me to try and forget who I was. It was ruinous advice. It
is only by realizing what I am that I have found comfort of
any kind. Now I am advised by others to try on my release
to forget that I have ever been in a prison at all. I know
that would be equally fatal. It would mean that I would
always be haunted by an intolerable sense of disgrace,
and that those things that are meant for me as much as
for anybody else—the beauty of the sun and moon, the
pageant of the seasons, the music of daybreak and the
silence of great nights, the rain falling through the leaves,
or the dew creeping over the grass and making it silver—
would all be tainted for me, and lose their healing power,
and their power of communicating joy. To regret one's
own experiences is to arrest one's own development. To
deny one's own experiences is to put a lie into the lips of
one's own life. It is no less than a denial of the soul."
—Oscar Wilde

"Lord, make me an instrument of Thy peace;
Where there is hatred, let me sow love;
Where there is injury, pardon;
Where there is error, the truth;
Where there is doubt, the faith;

Where there is despair, hope;
Where there is darkness, light;
And where there is sadness, joy.
O Divine Master,
Grant that I may not so much seek
To be consoled, as to console;
To be understood, as to understand;
To be loved as to love.
For it is in giving that we receive;
It is in pardoning that we are pardoned;
And it is in dying that we are born to eternal life."
—St. Francis of Assisi

"These pains you feel are messengers. Listen to them."
—Rumi

"Every single human being should be the fulfillment of a prophecy: for every human being should be the realization of some ideal, either in the mind of God or in the mind of man."
—Oscar Wilde

"Yield and overcome ... empty and be full ... have little and gain ... The sage embraces the One, and becomes exemplary to all the world. He is free from self-display, thus he shines; free from self-assertion, thus he is distinguished; free from boasting, thus his merit is acknowledged; free from self-complacency, thus he acquires superiority. Because he is free from striving, no one in the world can strive with him."
—Lao Tzu

"What matters is how quickly you do what your soul directs."
—Rumi

"People are often unreasonable and self-centered. Forgive them anyway.
If you are kind, people may accuse you of ulterior motives. Be kind anyway.
If you are honest, people may cheat you. Be honest anyway.
If you find happiness, people may be jealous. Be happy anyway.
The good you do today may be forgotten tomorrow. Do good anyway.
Give the world the best you have and it may never be enough. Give your best anyway.
For you see, in the end, it is between you and God. It was never between you and them anyway."
—Mother Teresa

"Abundance is not something we acquire. It is something we tune into."
—Dr. Wayne Dyer

"At the center of your being, you have the answer; you know who you are and you know what you want."
—Lao Tzu

"It is tragic how few people ever 'possess their souls' before they die. 'Nothing is more rare in any man,' says Emerson, 'than an act of his own.' It is quite true. Most people are other people. Their thoughts are someone else's opinions, their lives a mimicry, their passions a quotation."

—Oscar Wilde

"True emptiness is not empty, but contains all things. The mysterious and pregnant void creates and reflects all possibilities. From it arises our individuality, which can be discovered and developed, although never possessed or fixed."
—Jack Kornfield

"To know what you prefer, instead of humbly saying "Amen" to what the world tells you you ought to prefer, is to keep your soul alive."
—Robert Louis Stevenson

"It will be a marvelous thing—the true personality of man—when we see it. It will grow naturally and simply, flowerlike, or as a tree grows. It will not be at discord. It will never argue or dispute. It will not prove things. It will know everything. And yet it will not busy itself about knowledge. It will have wisdom. Its value will not be measured by material things. It will have nothing. And yet it will have everything, and whatever one takes from it, it will still have, so rich will it be. It will not be always meddling with others, or asking them to be like itself. It will love them because they will be different. And yet while it will not meddle with others, it will help all, as a beautiful thing helps us, by being what it is. The personality of man will be very wonderful. It will be as wonderful as the personality of a child."
—Oscar Wilde

~ Personal Notes ~

About the Author

Vince Calandra is a life-long student of philosophy and has been an executive at numerous technology companies, living both in the United States and abroad. His life experiences provide a highly intriguing life philosophy based upon purpose-driven life, universal forces, and guiding your life from a source of inner love.

Printed in the United States
By Bookmasters